SELECTED POEMS
KIRITI SENGUPTA

SELECTED POEMS
KIRITI SENGUPTA

Selected by DUSTIN PICKERING

TRANSCENDENT ZERO PRESS
HOUSTON, TEXAS

Published in the United States of America in August, 2025 by Dustin Pickering and Zachary Weiss, at Transcendent Zero Press, 16429 El Camino Real Apt. #7, Houston, Texas 77062-5786

Email: Editor@transcendentzeropress.org
Website: www.transcendentzeropress.org

All rights reserved. No part of this publication may be reproduced or transmitted (other than for purposes of review) in any form or by any means, electronic or mechanical, including photocopy, recording, or any information storage and retrieval system without the prior permission in writing from the publisher or the copyright holder where applicable.

Cover Design: **Bitan Chakraborty**
bitanchakraborty.com

ISBN-13: 978-1-946460-66-0 (Hardback)
978-1-946460-65-3 (Paperback)

Library of Congress Control Number: 2025942302

Copyright © Kiriti Sengupta 2025

Price: US Dollars 19.00 | INR 750/-

Distributed in India by **Hawakal** (hawakal.com)

for
Sanjeev Sethi

CONTENTS

The Poetry for an Age	9
Beyond the Eyes—a Preface	17
My Glass of Wine (2013)	23
The Reverse Tree (2014)	35
Healing Waters Floating Lamps (2015)	43
The Earthen Flute (2016)	63
Reflections on Salvation (2016)	87
Solitary Stillness (2017)	101
Rituals (2019)	119
Water Has Many Colors (2022)	155
Oneness (2024)	195
New Poems (from 2024 to 2025)	213

THE POETRY FOR AN AGE
PUBLISHER'S NOTE

Thematically, this volume reflects the stylistic shifts and evolving perceptions observed in Kiriti Sengupta's most compelling poems over the years. Poems from his early collections have been minimally edited for clarity. Starting with his initial bestselling trilogy—*My Glass of Wine*, *The Reverse Tree*, and *Healing Waters Floating Lamps*—I carefully selected representative works from each of his poetic offerings. Kiriti Sengupta appears as a wounded yet authoritative voice in verses such as "The Source," a poem that questions the processes of birth and death. This inquiry is addressed through an analogy: "They are as fragrant / and fresh / as the ancient fruit," he writes. The poetry depicting place is also featured in this volume. Poems like "Evening Varanasi" celebrate India's spiritual capital, Varanasi.

"The water here is not
a fire extinguisher.
Flames rise through the water."

The elements of fire and water represent the power of flowing divine energies. The poet's early work indicates his self-assurance within the craft. The strength of this poetry's language is rooted in traditional values and classical imagery. Starting with the *Appraisals* volume of criticism in 2017, I came to know Kiriti Sengupta through his literary persona. The phrase "cryptic idioms" was created to describe his style of composition. It perhaps refers to the cultural sensitivity embedded in his ambiguous use of language. It was in *Appraisals* that I first described Sengupta as a "radical traditionalist," meaning his ability, typical of metamodern thought, to critique dominant faith traditions while still respecting the tradition itself. *Reflections on Salvation*, published the year before *Appraisals*, introduced this category of consideration. *Reflections* belongs to the recent genre "flash wisdom," a term coined by Dr Mary Madec of Ireland. Flash wisdom is partly anecdotal, partly "cryptic idiom" that marks the boundary between the ancient world and our modern era of rapid industry and technological advancement.

However, flash wisdom is not social or political; it is, indeed, poetic. It is ambiguous and invites the reader to consider what these traditions mean in a modern context. For example, in "Stagecraft," the poet writes, "The pleasure of exploring and discovering the unknown comes only through the eyes, ears, nose, tongue, or skin." This opens spirituality to the senses, aligning with the stark reality of the physical world, which is sometimes denied in spiritual pursuits. *Reflections* is a collection aimed at modernising our understanding of ancient truths. In a 2025 interview with *Asymptote Journal*, Sengupta states, "So, although the verse perplexes readers, they should find its real meaning veiled underneath the surface. All holy texts are multi-layered, and the beauty lies in unfurling the truths from rigorous studies and practice."

I wrote the foreword to *The Earthen Flute* in 2016, highlighting one piece ("Let the Flowers Bloom") as a "tiny masterpiece." The sociocultural connections of the prose poem are one aspect of the poet's mysterious writing. As a critic, I suggested the poem reflected on the political differences between Bangladesh and India. However, the poem stands on its own merits as a beautifully crafted story. Lines of poetry flow simply and directly, "A white Lotus turns red as the Sun rises high in the sky." Although Sengupta is mainly known for his brevity, this prose poem is one of several longer works that speak volumes through symbolism. Lorna Dee Cervantes, a poet from the United States, writes of *The Earthen Flute*, "These poems dwell in a language beyond the many borders of languages." Sengupta's cosmopolitanism is symbolic—it reflects the modern issue of the "global village." In this internet era of attention-grabbing stakes, shallow consumerism, immediate gratification, and fake entrepreneurship, Sengupta's poetry shows a need for reflection. He isn't afraid to critique the modern world. His aesthetic choices, though instinctive and involuntary, provide the fast-paced post-capitalist audience with a sense of nature's rhythm: simplicity, beauty, harmony, and gratitude. *Solitary*

Stillness offers the most vital maxim, perhaps:

> "And then you can see the resurrected spirit
> approaching your stillness
> and challenging the world
> to leave you alone!" ("Quietude and Loneliness")

These lines reflect the modern dilemma with reflective anger and independence. Although birth rates are falling worldwide, human society still heightens tensions in the solitary human experience. This poem advocates a spirit that defends the right to be alone and at peace.

His appreciation of femininity is admirable and reflective. It contrasts with the cultural trend of the incel, a movement of men who blame women for male infertility. While this is a minority movement, it has gained momentum and attention in recent years. Historically, femininity is often objectified for physical allure rather than appreciated for its depth. In *Rituals*, the poem "The Unclad God" serves as the poet's stark personal confession, revealing his evolving attitudes towards bodily nudity. The poet writes, "I now look beyond the flesh, bone and keratin. // I've been told / the finer body dwells undressed." The title suggests spiritualised humanism, where the bare physical human becomes godlike. These final lines imply privacy but also ambiguously refer to the spiritual body of a person, which "dwells undressed." The essence of personhood is embraced. Sengupta also celebrates the feminine within the context of motherhood. Motherhood is not solely a human trait; Mother Earth is also part of the subtext. Sengupta writes in "Womb" from *The Earthen Flute*: "With every earthquake, I realize / I have failed to pay / enough attention / to my mother. / She has the right / to take me back into her," reflecting also on death. In "Mother Water" from the same book, he writes, "Ganga has her stories to tell / Wish she had someone to listen to her." The Ganges, India's holy river, is personified as struggling while we ignore her hardships. "Physiologists say the womb can withstand / much stress, and strain" reveals the poet's sensitivity. His reaction to the Covid pandemic is duly recorded with the collection *Water Has Many Colors*. "Boris Johnson in Isolation" and "Hibiscus" reflect the fear, the need for healing and medicine, and the loneliness of the sudden shift in social relations during the Covid era. "Hibiscus," in particular, shows the opportunity universally offered through the pandemic.

> "Feed the earth water
> she flows in abundance.
> Allow the planet to breathe:
> the air is her consort."

"Boris Johnson in Isolation" recognizes the hubris of the leadership in containing the deadly coronavirus. Most recently in his career, Sengupta compiled the pamphlet *Oneness*, which contains poignant eulogies and short pieces accompanied by visual art by Pintu Biswas. "On Exit" is a touching piece on the nature of grief. In "Man in the Rain," the cryptic character still resonates:

"Drenched in the deluge,
I progress to catch him.
He briskly drifts away.
My cellphone beeps:

The weather forecast suggests
a day-long cloudburst."

Time's ambiguities are questioned. Why is the weather forecast brought to the poet's attention after he experiences the actual rainstorm? The poem externalizes reality and brings it closer to an understanding of real and actual moments for the reader.

In an interview with *The Statesman*, Sengupta stated, "One may be a famous poet, a popular poet, an esteemed poet, an unknown poet, a non-practicing poet, but they all are poets in the first place. They are neither good nor bad. You love a poet, but do you love all his/her poems? I mean, all poems that he/she writes? You read a not-so-good poem, written by your beloved poet; how would you rate/grade the poet now?" This compels the reader to consider Sengupta's ability to navigate poetics without confounding the artist in the art, as well as his approach towards democratic acceptance.

In the *Asymptote Journal* interview, he says: "[…] perhaps I sought to reach out to readers who wished to interpret my poems quickly." This reflects his intention to be read in the modern world, where attention spans are increasingly short. Considering this comment on his shift poetically in *Oneness*, his comment reflects someone conscious of aesthetic choices and their effects on readers. In his later verses, as they develop, Sengupta becomes more lucid.

I carefully selected poems not as a "best of" compilation but as one that reflects these qualities of Sengupta as a poet evolving with and within our times. In one critical essay, I suggested Sengupta is a democratic voice who embraces the right to challenge consensus. Over the nearly decade I have known Kiriti Sengupta as a poet, I have served as editor, critic, and sounding board for his poetry. His poetry is contemporary, metamodern, and flows with the river of time.

This volume also features Sengupta's eight recent poems that have not been previously collected: "Violence," "Demonstration," "Fellowship," "Her Sacred Mist," "Photography," "Consciousness," "Durva," and "Eulogy." Some of these poems address recent events. "Violence" pertains to Rushdie's autobiography, *Knife*, and conveys a broader truth than Rushdie himself can articulate. "Fellowship" refers to a recent terrorist attack on Indian civilians, which led to a skirmish between Pakistan and India. "Demonstration" concerns the rape of a doctor at RG Kar Medical College and the subsequent "Take Back the Night" protests. These poems demonstrate that poets are not merely passive spectators of society but also proud catalysts within it. They respond to the world with creative passion.

Through this selected volume, I present the world of literary tradition with Kiriti Sengupta's continual development. His poetry acts as both a response to and a questioning of our modern era. Maintaining a balance between commitment to justice and spiritual exploration is vital for poetry to remain relevant and eternal. I extend my gratitude to the global readership.

Dustin Pickering
Founder, Transcendent Zero Press
July 2025
Houston, Texas

Beyond the Eyes—a Preface

> [...] नाटक करना बड़ी मुश्किल चीज़ है। इसलिए सिर्फ दीवाने करते हैं आजकल ... नाटक के लिए फ्री शो होना पड़ता है; तब ऑडियंस आती है। या पासेस होने पड़ते हैं, तब ऑडियंस आती है...
> — रत्ना पाठक शाह

> ... Doing plays nowadays is difficult. Only crazy people attempt them... It's necessary to offer free shows to draw an audience; otherwise, there must be free tickets...
> — Ratna Pathak Shah
> (eminent actor and theater personality)

The situation is quite similar when it comes to poetry and poets. When you ask poets, they will respond differently to the concern. Clearly, they are more invested in their poetry, but if they are not genuinely concerned about who reads their poems, then why do they get excited about publishing books? Few poets are committed to the art, while most see poetry as a benign leisure activity. Evidently, for them, "consumption" is not something they consider.

The situation is different when someone not only writes but also publishes others without charging a fee. Poetry also needs financial support! Poets should be paid for their work—that's easier said than done. Who will pay them? If you want to blame the publisher, I'd ask how that is possible if the community relies on free copies.

Who reads poetry these days? Who purchases poetry collections? These questions aren't intended to discourage poets. Rather, poets should humbly connect with readers and other poets to spread their work more widely. The Darwinian principle of "survival of the fittest" also applies to them.

For me, it's more important to explore what I am writing than why or how I am drawn to it. I find it crucial to understand the legacy and lineage of poetry written in the English language. It's a challenging task, seemingly impossible, no doubt. However, writing a poem just for the sake of it has never appealed to me. Never ever.

Mitali Chakravarty, a poet in her own right and a skilled editor, interviewed me for the January 2025 edition of *Borderless Journal*. She asked, "Why did you switch professions—from a dentist to a poet-publisher? What compulsion made you turn from a lucrative to an uncertain profession?" Although I explained my perspective in detail, it was clear she was not completely satisfied with my answer. As I showed her the draft of *Selected Poems*, she probed it again, "I was thinking—why don't you write about what drew you to poetry…I would have loved to learn about the urge that drove you to take the plunge. You just mentioned the circumstance in your interview, but not the intensity of the urge—what made your urge intense? [...] it is the most intriguing thing about your poetry—the depth of your poetry, I think, comes from that...I think about these things, but I have no solid conclusions."

Addressing Mitali's interest isn't easy: What draws me to poetry? What deepens my desire to indite poems? Poetry generally takes less reading time but demands more focus for reflection. Contemplation is a complex mental activity that calls on our hearts for help. Among all art forms, I find poetry most compelling. I feel free when I depict traditions in a contemporary way. Whether it's the Indian heritage I am deeply connected to or my Bengali upbringing, they illume me to express the unseen treasures of Bengali-Indian lives—values worth exploring in world literature. I remember the brief description of James Wright's *Selected Poems*: "Edited and with an introduction by Wright's widow, Anne, and his close friend, the poet Robert Bly, who also wrote an introduction, *Selected Poems* is a personal, deeply considered collection of work with pieces chosen from all of Wright's books. It is an overdue—and timely—new view of a poet whose life and work encompassed the extremes of American life."

As my publisher, Dustin Pickering—also a talented poet—prepares to release my *Selected Poems*, I observe he has carefully chosen pieces spanning over twelve years, from 2013 to 2025. I believe disciplined readers will interpret my poems in various ways. However, only time will reveal the truth.

I'm grateful to all my publishers, editors, and the periodicals that have published my work over the years: *The Common, The Florida Review Online, Moria Online, Headway Quarterly, The Lake, Grey Sparrow Journal, Amethyst Review, Dreich, Otoliths, Indian Literature, The Chakkar, Outlook, Borderless Journal, Madras Courier, The Daily Star*, among others.

I hope you find my work deserving of your time and attention.

Thank you!

Kiriti Sengupta
17 July 2025
New Delhi

Reference: https://us.macmillan.com/books/9780374529024/selectedpoems/

Twice-born

1
Who is the newborn:
the infant or the mother?

2
He cradles the neonate.
Fatherhood begins.

3
Guru initiates the lessons.
The disciple pursues the source.

4
Wearing a sacred thread, the boy responds
as the mantra resonates.

MY GLASS OF WINE

Year of Publication 2013
Publisher: Author's Empire Publications Pvt. Ltd. (New Delhi)
Illustration: Marut Kashyap

CONTENTS

The Source **27** | Blood Related **28** | The Air **30** | In Tune **31** | Wide **32** | I **33**

The Source

For years, I've been searching
for the flavors
of birth and death.

Do they exude the same?

They are as fragrant
and fresh
as the ancient fruit.

Blood Related

It was not branded, but a homemade wine.
Intimately divine,
I drank it first
after I was spiritually baptized.
Ah! My olden golden days of North India.
I often wondered why
the wine was made and offered!

I have been corrupt.

The Hindu *Tantrics* prefer the sight
of red light.
Be it of the attire,
or the holy sacrifice.

In the conventional practice of Islam,
Qurbani is a popular station.

You and I—
the Father and the Son—

the legacy goes on.
Inevitable, impeccable,
blood relation.

The Air

No one knew it was your
border vermilion that
made me kiss.
Although stark,
it seemed a magical bliss.

No one knew it was your
brown iris that stored
the pupil blue.
They called it
my instinct's hue.

No one knew I worshiped you
with my flaming heart.
No matter if I had a flower white,
you were to fly
like a passing kite.

In Tune

Remaining under self-control—
the tongue and the heart have fallen in love.
Look, zeroize them—
be a bird!

Wide

On the ascending shoots,
your fear matures,
and a few apprehensions too.

Your roots hold them tighter,
desperately deeper,
but much deeper rests your God.

My Glass of Wine

I

As identical as "I"
through the slice
of my sigh—

like the sky,
where the stars shine
and the Sun "I."

THE
REVERSE
TREE

Year of Publication 2014
Publisher: Moments Publication (Ahmedabad)
Illustration: Tamojit Bhattacharya

CONTENTS

Crisis **39** | Reversal—Reverse All **40**

Crisis

I have matched my lips
with the highs of your water
as you flowed joy.
The sun dares to surface
on your mirror, playing both
a *she*, and a *he* toy.

I've my own equation of love.
My *he* throbs in fire,
while my *she* is coy.

My girl shivers at times.
She is frank, but shy.
She hugs me with deep passion,
wetting me with her thin soy.

Empowered by the ray,
I worship the sun.
My *she* gives her all,
my *he* turns gay.

Reversal—Reverse All

1

numerous branches of the root
unite into two soft halves
some creases fine facing the sky
here the sun fails to light
the cloud fails to moisten
nature shelters the root
secures within an encapsulating tough skin

the shoot is long and thick
smoother skin palpating beneath
no study of the plants but of humans
the word of mouth
calls upon true reversal

2

defining soul is difficult
rather impossible

i have no doubt
i can perceive "i" in every decibel

my take is simple
it attracts dust
that smears the steps
to the body temple

i press two fingers firmly
on my ears
let the light dazzle
my imprisoned candle

i walk early morning
wrapped in fresh silk
air entices
my skin shivers
i hear sounds of click

in all works imperishable
i listen to the unheard

bundles of joy
drops of eyes
make "i" a bard

HEALING WATERS
FLOATING LAMPS

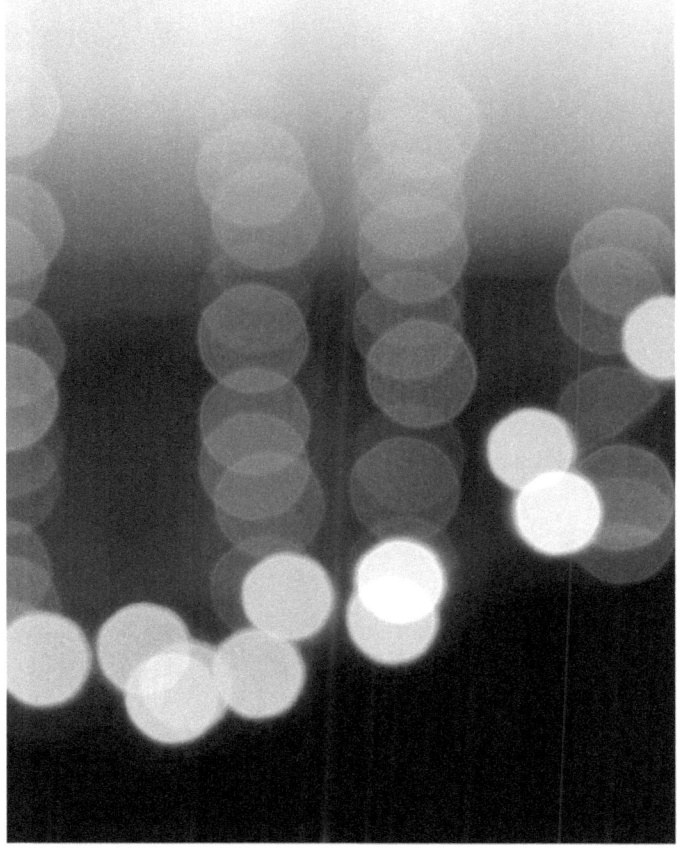

Year of Publication 2015
Publisher: Moments Publication (Ahmedabad)
Photograph: Arindam Chowdhury & Somnath Chatterjee

CONTENTS

Beyond the Eyes **47** | After Bath **48** | Evening Varanasi **49** | River of Tears **50** | Unravel **51** | In Dusty Feet **52** | Eyes of a Yogi **53** | Clarity **54** | Namesake **55** | Mellifluous Cry **57** | Celluloid **58** | Fish-Lip **59** | Closed-circuit **60** | Give Me More of Life **61** | Since Time Unknown **62**

Beyond the Eyes

I reach for the sky
as I draw a circle in the water.

Looking at the image,
I take a dip.

After Bath

I've bathed your feet with the water of the Ganges.
Last dip in the late afternoon,
I paid my first obeisance,
while my body was smeared with earthen mud.

I walked down the broken stairs
with a stony heart.
One step down, and down again…

I cannot learn swimming—
I'm scared even now.

I would not offer a homage anymore
as I offered prayers for the last time.

O Sun, I remember
I've bathed your feet
with the water of the Ganges.

Evening Varanasi

Have you seen floating lamps
on the river?

The water here is not
a fire extinguisher.
Flames rise through the water.

Prayers reach
the meditating Lord.

Note: In Varanasi (also known as Kashi), Lord Shiva is worshiped with great devotion, and in the evening, devotees place tiny lamps in the Ganges.

River of Tears

They have flowed over our eyes.
Afraid of being seen,
they are shy.

Despite their roomy eyes
they are blind.

They don't realize—
not all rivers succeed in uniting.

Unravel

The rear desks are clean.
The thriving crowd relishes
fast food, lawsuits.

Healers worry about the front.
It is dusty, empty but advocates
spiritual pursuits.

My Master enjoys the stage.
Looking at the sparkling crowd, he says:
Reach the void and see the cage.

In Dusty Feet

I was about to prostrate,
but refrained from paying an obeisance
to my enlightened Master.
His great toes housed
holy grains of dust.
He took good care of his feet.
I picked the grains quickly
to place them on my head.

I followed his footsteps,
even along the filthy roads.
I wished to become such devout grains
to stay attached to his feet forever.

I turned back as I failed.
I could not hold the grains
on my big toes.

God remained thumb-sized
with dusty feet.

Eyes of a Yogi
remembering Sri Ramakrishna Paramahansa

A mother bird quietly sits on her eggs.
Her eyes appear distantly
connected to the world.

Hey, look at them—
tiny wings!
The mother transforms into the sky.

Clarity

I have seen my mother
preparing ghee out of milk.
She never used butter
to clarify it further.

She'd boil and store the milk
in large quantities for days.
Once cooled, she'd separate
thick layers of yellow froth.
Layer after layer, she filled
the storage pot, then put it on
the burner, which filled
the house with aromatic milk.

So organic is my memory—
the granular residue lifted us to heaven.
Ah! Pious Ghee, and incorrigible.

Namesake

1

Whispers the tale of our character—
color and its fragrance merge to call it a rose.
A lot matters
if we remember the name.

2

With sheer innocence, the boy told the story of his watching movies in a hall named "Nadia Talkies." Sharing the same story many a time, uttered the name, *talkies*, and had his face shine! Humble was the hall, so were its viewers. Alas! It's no more; it has been abolished by the estate promoters. The boy is now a grown-up man. Nadia remains inside its reel-can.

3

The womb carries water—so do your eyes.
Water builds the fetus

that becomes "I."
It's a room for the eyes
under the name "Rely."

4

Carrying myself is significant indeed.
Crucifixion is Christ-filled.
As I remember,
my mind turns candle-lit.

They pinned it before.
Will do that now and again.
No arrangements of incense…

God and life—
moving apart.

Mellifluous Cry

The labor room was busy,
especially the midwife.
She was unhappy
with the silence of the newborn.

Much worried about it,
she patted the back of the infant.
Doula screamed in frustration:
Hey, cry out!

On the other side of the closed door,
the father was eager to hear his baby.
He was all set to smile and celebrate
the first communication.

Celluloid

Gold is precious and so is the time
we spent together—from the morning tea
through the lavish lunch, until you said,
Signing off for today.

I was hesitant.
I never said goodbye.

Signs are private.
I keep my eyes open
round the clock.

Fish-Lip

I've read the morphology
of the fish-lip
gives a hint of the water color deep down.

A small aquarium in my living room—cornered—
marks of love and kisses on either side.
My lips are thin with no traces of color, but water.

Closed-circuit

If it had not been fragile,
I would have placed
a camera upon my collarbone.

And then
I would have taken out
the extra lenses one by one.

Ah! Such impeccable
folds of civilization.

Give Me More of Life

Amusing, but it's real.

A young girl was standing
at the riverbank, her hands
holding a live *koi*.
I was curious, and she said,
Hold it and you will understand.
She ran away, flashing a quick smile.

I surfed through the radio channels
on my cellphone.
I heard a commentary on the *Gita;*
a speech on the *Visvarupa Darshan*.

The cellphone blinked,
I saw a message my friend sent.
A famous line by Tagore—
Chokher aaloy dekhechilem chokher bahire.
(*I envisioned the external through the light of my eyes.*)

Note: *Koi* is a fish that survives for a few hours when kept out of water. In Bengali, a girl's life is colloquially called a *Koi*'s life, as they can endure all the dangers they face.

Since Time Unknown

I have not reached yet
the science of you. I know
I'm glued to, and stand still
with some fixations.
Since time unknown
you spin and continue to swivel.
You have a firm grip.

Faulty are my limbs,
they tilt even on the steady floor.
I realize it is all in my mind
as the sky swings.

You spin and continue to swirl
since periods unknown.

THE EARTHEN FLUTE

Year of Publication 2016
Publisher: Hawakal (New Delhi, Calcutta)
Illustration: Tamojit Bhattacharya

CONTENTS

Keep an Eye **67** | Womb **68** | Moon—The Other Side **69** | Kajal Deeghi **70** | Experience Personified **71** | Gateway to God **72** | Time and Tide **73** | Clues to Name **74** | Cryptic Idioms **76** | Seventh Heaven **79** | Let the Flowers Bloom **81** | Mother Water **84**

Keep an Eye

Among the three eyes of Durga,
the third one has remained
the same over the ages.

It has been kept open:
either full or half.

Sculptors never bothered;
they've only experimented
on her earthly eyes.

Womb

With every earthquake, I realize
I have failed to pay
enough attention
to my mother.
She has the right
to take me back into her.

I know she will take
as much care
as she did before.

World, you may comment on material loss,
only the mother understands her rupture pain.

Moon—The Other Side

Memories unveil themselves through snapshots;
the moon has its glory
pinned in poetry.

Elegance, marks of disgrace—you may argue—
not all can be hunky-dory with brushes
soaked in the colors of passion and hunger.

Can you remember the bread
Sukanta left behind?
It was baked under the full-moon light.

A tombstone might request flowers and tears,
while hunger can only be satisfied
with food to eat.

If you can recall, the moon has its share of crevices,
allowing restricted entry of light,
love and joy.

Note: Sukanta Bhattacharya was a Bengali poet and a key figure in modern Bengali poetry. His poetry is marked by social rebellion, patriotism and humanism. In a poem "Hey Mohajibon" ("O, Great Soul"), Sukanta wrote: "A world affected by hunger is too prosaic; the full moon resembles a toasted bread."

Kajal Deeghi

Leisure around the water;
it was named Kajal Deeghi.

I was inquisitive;
water here didn't look black,
nor would I call it green.
The lake seemed deep.
I quickly recalled *Banalata Sen*.
Her profound eyes resembled
a bird's nest.
Those eyes—the water in the lake—
they house, and reflect.

Note: A Deeghi (lake) is a naturally formed body of water. Kajal is a widely used color by Asian women to define their eyes. "Banalata Sen" (বনলতা সেন) is a widely read Bengali poem by Jibanananda Das, one of the revered poets in Bengali literature. Banalata Sen has become a symbol of the captivating mystery of femininity, embodying eternal beauty and profound love.

Experience Personified

As I walk through an abandoned playground,
I see new grasses bathed
in the dew of dawn.
Putting off my shoes,
I stand barefoot and walk again.

Tiny droplets envelop my feet
and permeate the toes.
I don't call it a feeling,
I will name it
my experience.

Gateway to God

Prayers carry lives within.
They are the expressions
our desires take refuge in.

Despite all worldly pleasures and fulfillment,
we remain scared.
Wishes are chanted with closed eyes.

And we continue to live being frightened.
Like inevitable death,
an enormous God steps in.

Time and Tide

It was 8 am, and the butler inquired, "What would you like for your breakfast, Sir?" We had partied the night before with a group of young ladies. I cautiously ordered a slice of bread and a cheese omelet. I overheard the boy instructing a woman cook. It was an open kitchen layout, and I saw a Bengali widow in her late forties placing the bread in the toaster. She set the timer and quickly picked two eggs from the basket. I noticed her eyes as she broke the eggs.

The boy served me breakfast on a white dish. The bread was perfect, but the omelet looked odd. I realized that the woman did not whisk the yolks properly. Slightly annoyed with the service, I asked the waiter, "Is she a new appointee?" He hesitantly replied, "She is my aunt, Sir. She lives in our ancestral home. Aunt lost her husband when she was only eighteen!"

Clues to Name

1

An experiment I undertook. A seed slept in the dark, clueless—no viable chant—what if awakened by a mantra? A syllable to prefix and suffix, and thus was my pride and prejudice. I was confined, even as I longed to move on. The pride was dear; dearer than my dearest.

2

Following a cunning way, I was keen to taste some greatness. A tree stood with its green veil. Through its branches, I noticed the ascent of sap, but it had no salt. Some names are sweet, some seeds are added at the source.

3

As one finds it apt. Just the way the mind seeks. My mind. Mantra bears lust. Petty you, you blame the luster! Lust reinstated—inevitable it is.

4

Immersion via the mirror—goodbye to the goddess, but the lion keeps awake with closed eyes. His eyes are terrific—mesmerizing, or giving all as I surrender. The first involves mixing, while the latter denotes craving.

Deviations bring popularity and endless celebrations. Fists full of water and free donations—serving the pilgrims. Withdrawal is reversed.

5

Complete a bath and a full dip—no excuses, please. You sprinkle drops—your wisdom runs into the lustrous hole. Wet hands do not burn incense, they say. Prohibited it is. Water has no call, no décor either; it floats the bone and the ash free.

Cryptic Idioms

reflections on Patanjali's Yoga Sutras

1

I say Yama,
and you think of the God of Death.

I say Yama,
but I meant the rules of restraint.

Contemplating worldly loss
is dispassionate.

2

Disgusted, you wrote,
when I asked you to fill in the blank.

Too many laws shape a life.
You could have written: Hell.

Isn't it the place where Yama dwells?
A balanced blend makes a delicious cocktail.

3

You have been practicing
postures for health and fun.
Kali never fails to protrude
her long, bloody tongue.

4

A flute plays along the serpentine track.
Breathing tunes it from mute to high to crack.

Over eons, religion and its absence
appear back-to-back.

5

Withdrawal has its symptoms,
like an illness.

They both demand care;
they prefer the countryside over a metropolis.

6

Marketing began with the inception
of communication.

Not a gimmick, but Yoga is now
at its creative best.

Patanjali must be happier,
I bet.

Endorsement suggests:
"An idea can change your life!"

7

Many struggle to envision the self—
a mirror shatters to break the dreams.

Not lenses or a pair of glasses,
but thick skin that keeps my eye covered.

And I patiently await the unveiling.
Trust me, the eye can see.

No sorrows, nor a hint of delight;
a wonderful world opens up deep inside.

Seventh Heaven

1

Justifications for earthly and underground matters sound clichéd. Earth is where I wish to live, but Padmavati prefers her home beneath the ground. One of the obstacles is "hell." The mosquitoes, flies, and even the butterflies cause trouble.

2

Let them be; never mind if they are cheap. Do you find proverbs demanding? "I won't even try the lane that does not lead to your home"—no matter if you say this several times, my heart beats abnormally. It won't listen to other lines. It won't say anything either.

3

I'll now walk along the road; what about you? Hold my hands and take me with you—enough of your so-called innocence. Look at the roadside plaque; it says: "Wait for a minute here, o' trespassers." Don't tell me your legs ache as you climb the stairs to heaven. Don't you bear love in your soul?

4

In Radha's name, your love has condensed. The peacock's tail leaves a mark on Radha's forehead. Will you blame the traffic every time you arrive late?

5

I'm not a deviant! I'm a woman as long as I'm dynamic. I'm a woman unless I'm still. What do you think of a woman's voyage to heaven?

6

My soul seeks, but the eyes fail to see. They remain closed at the final destination. It is a habit. I can now rest and relax for a while.

Is it morning?

7

Much excitement prevails. It feels like I'm inside an insulated tube, and my heroine attracts and sings.

Why wouldn't Radha be annoyed?

Let the Flowers Bloom

1

Elderly Mujibar has no money; he owns a hovel and a large pond. Mujibar eats rice and boiled Shapla as he returns from work. He cultivates Shapla in the pond, which also contains Lotus. Mujibar picks both the flowers and keeps them in bunches before selling them at the market. His five-year-old son does not understand which bunch will be used in their kitchen, and what goes into the Hindu household.

2

A white lotus turns red as the Sun rises high in the sky. Mujibar has no idea about what is happening and considers it a phenomenon. His little son rushes to the veranda and stretches his brown arms in the sunlight.

3

Leaving his little son alone, Mujibar dies of uncontrolled fever. In the afternoon, the young boy wanders around the paddy field, and in the morning, he works in the tea stall beside his hut. He serves tea in small glasses to the customers.

4

The boy grows up; people call him Robi. On a cold winter morning, a fakir arrives at the tea kiosk. He does not have warm clothing. Robi approaches the fakir, "My father has given me a roof, but I have no sky to look at."

5

The fakir offers a tiny copper box—a sacred *tabeez*. He suggests, "Chain it around your neck, my son!" Robi protests, "Hey, you gave me a piece of copper while I asked for the sky?" The fakir urges enthusiastically, "Come on, it is filled with my prayers. I have given you a mountain, my boy. Break through the roof you have."

6

No magic, just pure trust soaked in innocence! Robi no longer works; he spends endless days in his hut, cherishing the holy mountain. The roof remains as it is; the moon does not show up. A piece of the sky doesn't even appear despite Robi's constant longing for it. He holds the tabeez tightly in his hand, and while staring at the roof, he whispers, "I won't offer you a drape if I don't get a bird."

7

A bird flutters its wings, and the sound is quite familiar. Not a crow nor a heron—an unknown bird. It continues standing on the mud pad. A few flowers are visible, and they are not Shapla. Robi feels warmth, especially along the spine, as if a sudden surge of hot water is flowing up the spinal duct!

8

A fragrant ambience settles in as the bird soars into the air. Robi's face gets splattered with drops of mud from the flying bird. A handful of soil, and the hut is flooded with sunlight streaming through the broken roof. Robi feels much warmer now. A milkman knocks on the door, "Collect milk in the can, *chacha*!"

Note: Shapla (Water Lily) is the national flower of Bangladesh. The flower and its stem are edible. A tabeez is a metallic case (square, rectangular, round, or oval in shape) that is believed to provide worldly benefits to its wearer. Lotus is the national flower of India, and it is used in Hindu households during religious rituals. Chacha is the brother of one's father.

Mother Water

Ganga has her stories to tell;
wish she had someone to listen to her.
The story of her arrival is passé
and so is her passage through the ages,
witnessing numerous banks of civilizations.

We are not even bothered to see her struggle.
She fights as boats ply on the river:
she accommodates them,
their load, and men.
Physiologists say the womb can withstand
much stress and strain.

Ganga listens to our prayers,
both mute and loud,
we wonder if she enjoys
the enchanting hymns
devotees sing with music and flowers.

People die—
we cremate them on Hindu pyres,

and float the ashes in the river.
Ganga absorbs all of them
as the residues settle into the soil
beneath her waters.

Ganga has her stories to tell;
wish she had someone to listen to her.
The story of her nursing the fetus
contained in an inflated uterus,
as she patiently awaits her tour,
accompanying new life.

Note: Ganga refers to the river Ganges, which is commonly worshiped by Hindus across the globe.

REFLECTIONS ON SALVATION

Year of Publication 2016
Publisher: Transcendent Zero Press (Houston, Texas)
Cover Illustration: Sourish Mitra

CONTENTS

Saffron **91** | Payment **92** | Stagecraft **93** | Cow **94** | Fire **95** | Paradise **96** | Krishna **97**| Detachment **98** | Bondage **99** | Salvation **100**

Saffron

Why do we hire a priest to worship the household gods? I wonder if we are not capable enough to do it ourselves. We are attached to the sacred thread, the holy *shaligram*, and we keep the idea of listening to loud chants of religious verses. Are we not cursed by ourselves?

Saffron adds color and flavor to certain delicacies, but when it appears on your attire, I perceive you as saintly and pious. It is all in my mind, which has been tuned to accept or reject the effects of the colors they contain.

With saffron comes renunciation, and with renunciation comes attachment. Attachment to the world, attachment to domesticity, or perhaps the gods.

How does one become a monk? Is it by renouncing the fruits of actions one undertakes? Even the gods invite dependence, and remember, they are considered superior to the saints.

Payment

Necessity is the mother of invention, they say! You are one of the requisites the gods look out for; they need you to prosper further, and look, you plan to invent them through renunciation? Ask them instead to leave your earthly existence, and then let them realize the value of attachment.

You seem determined to disregard the cause-and-effect relationship. You work to get paid. Your family awaits money on your payday. Does wisdom urge you to neglect your loved ones? Did it not advise you to love your neighbors?

Stagecraft

Lights, camera, action! The spot boy uses a clapstick while the director utters these words. The actors deliver what they are asked to do. They follow their director, and at times, improvise their actions.

You perform, and we call it a performance. Shakespeare said, "All the world's a stage." What if you have no audience? What if you are not applauded? You might blame your luck, but did you deliver your best? Salvation is but enlightenment, achievable only through actions and your sensory gateways.

The pleasure of exploring and discovering the unknown comes only through the eyes, ears, nose, tongue, or skin.

Cow

An astrologer advised me to donate a few lactating cows to our family priest. He believes that by donating cows, I will be able to rid myself of my accumulated sins and ultimately please the gods, securing prosperity, wealth, and peace.

I bought two cows and gave them to the priest. He appeared happy and blessed me, "I'm delighted and so are the gods." Although I followed the astrologer, my luck has not changed yet. Our priest seems disappointed as those cows have stopped giving milk.

If scriptures are made for humans, what about humanity?

Fire

You think of *yajña*, you consider liberation, but I think of the amount of ghee it consumes. I think of the number of trees it kills. The *Vedas* did not count on malnutrition; they did not even consider the environment, let alone poverty.

I wonder if the Vedic scriptures were written by a group of wise men who never lived on this earth. How can two give birth to one when they are poles apart?

Paradise

No matter if you sacrifice your sweat and blood or feel exhausted, you are to consider yourself duty-bound. You must perform *yajña*, donate, and meditate. Bhabapagla, the great philosopher, might have connected beauty to duty, but did he count on our appearance?

Roma spent her life on us—her children, husband, and her teaching career. Family has always been her highest priority. She neglected her health, ignored her basic needs and dreams. Ma has been suffering from psoriasis for over a decade, and she hates stepping out in the sun. She no longer looks pretty. Her skin is patchy. It itches, oozes blood, and aches. My mother still takes care of her family. I therefore ask Bhabapagla, is Roma heading for heaven because of duty or beauty?

Note: Doctrines of Bhabapagla at http://bhabapagla.com/doctrins.htm

Krishna

We won't be bound by our actions, whether good or bad—we are not the doers. So, when I'm worshipping the gods, they are, in fact, worshipping themselves. Why would I allow that? I would rather worship myself and find happiness. My physical body, the words I speak, and my mind—they all have one thing in common: "I."

No matter if someone commits an unfair act, the gods suffer through us, and so, we remain unaffected. Did you hear me? You might call me ignorant, but I am neither Krishna nor your beloved political servant.

Detachment

Marriages are made in heaven. But then, they too are expectant! Why wouldn't a couple dream of becoming parents to their child if they are capable of bringing new life into the world?

On a serious note, I plan to donate a few copies of the *Geeta* to infertility clinics. I would love to hear them advise: "Act, but forget!" The *Geeta* says, *karmaṇy-evādhikāras te mā phaleṣhu kadāchana / mā karma-phala-hetur bhūr mā te saṅgo 'stvakarmaṇi*—You have a right to perform your duties, but you are not entitled to the fruits of your actions. Never consider yourself to be the cause of the results of your activities, nor be attached to inaction.

But did I think about how a childless couple might react? Situations change, but scriptures stay the same. Mundane!

Note: The *Geeta* Chapter 2, Verse 47

Bondage

Even an ovum awaits communion to become a zygote. The organ gives birth and sacrifices one after another. If not fertilized, they flow away from the tract. You call it a monthly departure, but I would rather name it "link failure."

Salvation

Does one receive the gods? Even if they exist on the planet, I'll preferably inquire: "Get me the total headcount!" I can hear someone murmuring, "God is one and amorphous." See, it is God who claims: *sarva dharmān parityajya / mām ekaṁ śaraṇaṁ vraja*—*abandon all religions and take refuge in me.*

We live as long as we breathe, and it is only the breathing that occurs of its own will. No gods, but the breath that creates a home for our life and death.

They say that God dwells within; it is then the mortal exploration of the resort where salvation is largely seen!

Note: The *Geeta* Chapter 18, Verse 66

SOLITARY
STILLNESS

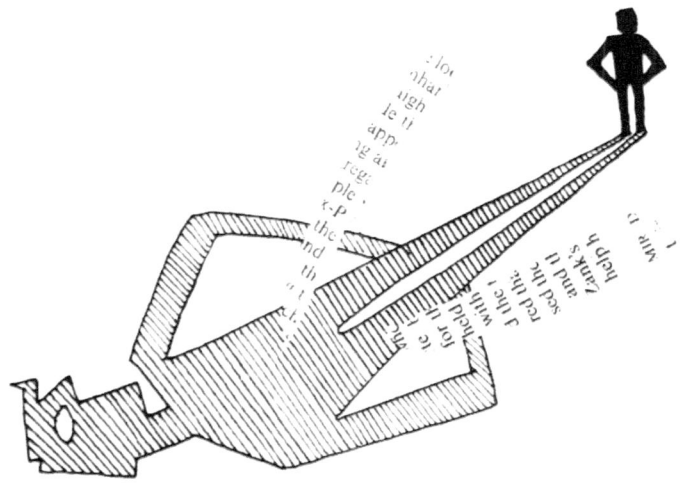

Year of Publication 2017
Publisher: Hawakal (New Delhi, Calcutta)
Illustration: Joyeeta Bose

CONTENTS

The Pilgrimage **105** | Quietude and Loneliness **106**| Tournesols **107** | Manhattan Skyline **108** | Illumination **110** | Write to Eat **111** | (Re)Formation **112** | Expressions **113** | Love Story **114** | In Conversation with **115** | The Pillars of Soil **116**

The Pilgrimage

Pipiray pak uthe moribar tore…

Phullara declares,
The ants develop wings to bring death.

Fire is not the reason.
Their flight, the pilgrimage.

Note: The well-known saying, "The ants develop wings to bring death," originates from the *Chandimangalkavya* by Mukundaram Chakraborty. Phullara, the wife of Kalketu, is a character in the medieval Bengali text. It is believed that, despite the inevitability of death, ants fly into fire out of ignorance.

Quietude and Loneliness

For God's sake, don't take silence for granted.
It is loud, hypnotic and overrated.
It has a spiritual world charm attached to it;
you never know if it will declare you dead.

And then you can see the resurrected spirit
approaching your stillness
and challenging the world
to leave you alone.

Tournesols
after Vincent van Gogh

Make them come alive, I said,
give them the sun and a parrot
if you think it's right.

At least some gay, yellow shine.
Wish he had listened to me
while he painted the sunflowers on canvas.

Life would not have become still
if there had been water in the vase.

Manhattan Skyline

I wasn't bothered
if the world thought differently
about Dylan's winning of the Nobel Prize.

I would not justify his long silence,
or if he was rude, as the Swedish Academy
was unable to reach him by phone.

Readers found out that
Dylan told the British paper,
"Amazing, incredible!"

No comments; it's better to stay quiet
and keep looking at the skyline—
the Manhattan Skyline.

Here lies an artist—here lies a union of two men:
one who sings
and one who strikes through the concrete lane.

Solitary Stillness

A breathtakingly vast sky
tinted with yellow, a bridge marks the horizon,
and below, the water mellows in pale sorrow.

No landscape but the infinite meets the brush;
mind becomes still,
while "traveling the back roads, freeborn style."

Note: *Manhattan Skyline* is one of the paintings by Bob Dylan, exhibited on November 5, 2016, at the Halcyon Gallery in New Bond Street, London. Dylan has written a preface to the exhibition catalog, which states that his works have "something to do with the American landscape" while "staying out of the mainstream and traveling the back roads, freeborn style."

Illumination

We were walking down the solitary lane,
from the bright end to the dark.
We, two men, saw twin selves—
though not in flesh—
the shadows.

They emerged from our mortal frames,
thinner, but didn't hesitate to grow longer
and even surpassed us as we marched ahead.
Our shadows cherished every bit of the lightlessness
until a sudden gush of glow bathed us.

Write to Eat

Do you mean regurgitation? I fear vomiting. Let the sac receive the food; I will allow my gut to absorb its vital nutrients. The world dislikes a vomiting neonate.

I lose words as I write; my pen loses ink with every word it puts down. Would you like me to withdraw the lines I sketched?

The ink has dried on the paper; the pot can't be refilled with scribbles. Do I now surrender my pen?

(Re)Formation

You either have a regular or irregular pulse. An irregular pulse can sometimes be in a regular rhythm, or you might have an irregularly irregular pulse. In all such situations, a person neither stops breathing nor living. A deviation from normalcy is not necessarily a sign of disease. You never know when your body accepts changes and makes them part of your natural constitution.

Expressions

A protest does not require our humble submission;
otherwise, we would have called it
an appeal to authority.

An appeal is not about being buried underground.
If it were,
we would name it a prayer to the Lord.

Did Jesus remain silent
when they nailed him
to the cross?

Love Story

Why does my photographer friend ask
the models to avoid greasepaint?

Camera reciprocates a mirror.
The mirror makes an impression
and exposes the concealment of flaws.

Camera mocks the disguise
and celebrates light.

In Conversation with

I have always enjoyed horror movies, but honestly, I was afraid of ghosts. Watching the first show of the day was a must, and if I failed, I cursed those around me. Every successful attempt disturbed our sleep. If I needed to go to the washroom, I would call Ma, "Keep awake until I come back." She remained watchful. After marriage, it has always been my wife.

Now, I have reached an understanding. I no longer seek company. To my complete bewilderment, if the ghost appears, I've decided to offer it a chair first, and then I'll plead, "Take a seat and relax! Let us share our stories."

The nights have never been so long before.

The Pillars of Soil

"There are several elephants up in the sky," a friend giggled. I remember we were studying in the first grade at our primary school. I believed her words until I learned about the science of rain—how the clouds collide and melt into drops—how the trees help in rainfall, and so on. By then, we had read about the incredible legends of Mia Tansen, the great maestro, and how he brought a shower while performing *Megh Malhar* in the royal court of the Mughal emperor Akbar.

On my way to an old-age home,
I witnessed the cloudburst once again.
The trees along the motorway
listened to the sound of rain
with their heads bowed.

As if the woods were enjoying
the gentle care they longed for.

As if the trees were paying attention
to the instructions sent from the sky.

They were probably being told that
the world would need another maestro
who could sing for the seasoned flesh—
those who walked the earth—
whose roots ran deep into the ground.

RITUALS

Year of Publication 2019
Publisher: Hawakal (New Delhi, Calcutta)
Illustration: Partha Pratim Das

CONTENTS

Comeback **123** | The Resurrection **124** | On the Richter Scale **125** | Appraisal **127** | When God is a Woman **128** | Accommodation **129** | The Expectant Mother **130**| Tradition **131** | The Blues **132** | Dentures **133** | From Being Late in Calcutta **134** | Gravity **136** | Patience **137** | The Stepwell **138** | Y-Gene **139** | Screenplay **141** | The Untold Saga **142** | The Unclad God **144** | Promising Griefs **146** | Anyday **147** | A Place Like Home **148** | Sridevi **149** | After the Book Fair **150** | Masala Muri **151** | Faith **153** | Exhibition **154**

Comeback

I return after a year. The room is full of dust, the floor smeared with thick silt; the mirror on the wall is glued to ripped paint, and it deceives. Several prominent lips on cups and plates…cigarette butts stick out from the water jar…the filth radiates an intimate odor. My tired eyes uncover the kohl of night, while my glasses spot tears. The fruit platter was in the storeroom—the leftovers ache—did someone split the cord of the earphone?

The Resurrection

Slumber unfolds its arms as it wakes up. The tiny particles scattered in the air absorb the sunlight; they seem to be delighted and drone the song of liberation. Sleep is now conscious, like the attraction between mother and her newborn.

Flawlessly arranged, the room is ready for hard work and is not yet marked by fatigue. At a distance, the mother awaits her demonstration in sweat and grime.

On the Richter Scale

1

It's drizzling since cockcrow. It won't stop. They name it the hallmark of the season. Winter precipitates. 4 on the Richter scale sits comfortably on the human body. A scattered crowd walks on the street. Roadside lamps romance with their acrylic veneers. Doused Banyan trees await desiccation. The west side of the footpath marks the ghettos. Here, the residues burn. Frozen limbs budge. Numb nerves wish to whistle.

2

Fleeing the house and leaving the doors ajar. Is it perversion or fallacy? To amble solitary in winter is amusing. It provides solace for some time. Smoke does not arise as the mouth opens. Tiny crystals of ice accumulate along the crease. They melt as the nip recedes, barring a hint of steam. An aberration? No trace of forgotten ventilators, the fumes swirl to ascend. The scale marks 5. Does vapor perspire?

3

A seven-year-old canvas invites dust bunnies. Mopping whitens it; gray patches lurk in the brightness. It looks at the artist, Desolation, who paints fresh watercolors. The cloth blushes. It absorbs all the cuddles. The elbow hits and makes it pale. The veil dissolves. A mirror bathes in glassy water to reflect light. The sea longs for a rendezvous. Desolation stands still. The Richter scale fails to respond.

Appraisal

1

Timing is crucial, to say the least.
Do you consider nature baffling?

We can certainly look up at the sun
at dawn and dusk, or when it rains.

2

Patrons do not frequent aging
accolades anymore. In a pristine
white bed, they have been resting
for ages. Several vases hold roses
on the bedside table, but refuse
to scent the décor. The flowers aren't dry;
they haven't shed petals either.

An appraiser is called out to rouse
commendation.

When God is a Woman

How many householders meet in
a whorehouse?

How many *mujras* dwell in a kotha?

How many neonates hew to a bordello?

Like her admirers
God is silent.
In her sinews,
hides a hint of soil
from the yard of courtesans.

Accommodation

Rain or moisture,
what do ferns long for?

Downpour evicts roots;
dampness helps them
settle on the rocks.

The Expectant Mother

She lies supine.
Close to her chest, she holds
a greased mango leaf,
blazed to kohl. Her eyes
whist like a whisper.

She stretches her hands
to douse the sky
with blood and water.

Tradition

I have no choice but to listen
to the same words again and again.
Neither am I aware of the consequences.
It is not cerebral but sensory.

Customs are like meditation—
worthy of unhurried contemplation.
Practice adds to their maturity,
I know servitude is congenital.

The Blues

The door is closed.
It is difficult to remember when
light entered the guardhouse.
In this heavy air,
how does one breathe?

As the gate opens wide,
I see a run for pleasure.
Horizon marks salvation.
Not in allegories,
but in eyes, lust flickers!

In extreme hunger,
how does one understand the economy?
Wants mask the subconscious.

Dentures

I prefer patients who are edentulous. I dread a tooth will wrangle my expertise, and I'll fail to make an impression.

From Being Late in Calcutta

As soon as you mark me late
I'll talk about events
that guide me to the records
you maintain.

I'd say crowded buses invite passengers
from unscheduled halts.
I'd emphasize the number of speed-breakers on road,
and their poor performance in preventing accidents.

I'd tell you trains run late.
Signals are laggy between stations.
I won't forget to mention how
a sudden protest
makes the train stand still for hours.

I'd discuss the day I reported late,
owing to the instantaneous suspension
of underground train services
as a man killed himself on the railway lane.

I'd ask you to remember why I came late the other day.

If you can recall,
I had indigestion despite eating at home.

I blamed farmers for sprinkling pesticides on crops.
I pointed at my salary that failed to buy organic veggies.

And then,
I'd invariably argue about maintenance and population.

I'd appreciate China, the one-child policy, and their claim on
how the government prevented four hundred million births.
And how India thrives on the revenues earned
from selling nicotine and condoms.

I'll explore other issues
the next time I'm late.

Gravity

The aircraft takes off.
First officer alerts,
The dismal climate may cause turbulence.

Upheavals follow air-pockets.

My scared son grips the armrests.
I comfort him, *Relax! Bumps help us
realize the earth.*

Patience

I advise my part-time assistant
not to quit his day job and
ignore all coercions.
He should calm his nerves.

I speak of the banyan tree
stemming from the exterior cornice.
Roots penetrate concrete
until they are excised.

The Stepwell

Kalapani insinuates servitude for a lifetime.

In the premises of Purana Qila,
the baoli is alive.

Eighty-nine stairs down,
water is yet to scour the shine.
It awaits liberation.

Note: A stepwell is called baoli, regionally.

Y-Gene

My friends were aware of the wish I nurtured.
If I had a daughter,
I would name her Srividya.
I was not influenced by any actor.
Our prayer room hosted a dazzling
crystal Sri Yantra on the holy altar.

My wife's desires were girly too.
She wished to drape her daughter
in frilly dresses.
She had plans to find her girl
a groom in clover, so my wife could
live comfortably. Prior to her labor,
my mother-in-law keenly observed
my wife's navel, *Come on, it's a boy!*

It was a boy, a cute little one
of two and a half kilos.
To take care of the borderline weight,
special supplements were arranged.

My wife looked proudly bright.
We worshiped the Narayana
right after the holy bath.

My son is at school.
It's a co-education convent.
After school he tells his mother,
Girls sit on the left side.

Screenplay

Death suggests how fruitless
it is to hold a grudge.
Life has ways to
recommence the soliloquy.

The Untold Saga

It took two hands
to kill Mahishasura.

Trishula was used
to destroy the demon.

Autumn accompanies
your ten-armed avatar.

Like many women,
you followed the husband.

You emerged from the gods.
You had several weapons!

The fiend was considered invincible.
You won the battle but did not claim the bounty.

That you are worshiped on earth
gave no relief to gasping Nirbhaya.

She was scourged by scoundrels
who dug into her body parts.

She followed death
thus could not create an epic.

Note: Nirbhaya died from fatal injuries following a gang-rape in Delhi in 2012. Mahishasura is a Sanskrit word composed of Mahisha (buffalo) and Asura (demon), indicating buffalo demon. As a demon, Mahishasura waged war against the gods. He was ultimately killed by Durga. It is an important symbolic legend in Hindu mythology, particularly Shaktism. The legendary battle of Mahishasura and Durga is narrated in many parts of South Asian and Southeast Asian Hindu temples, monuments and texts such as the Devi Mahatmya. Trishula is a trident, commonly used as the principal symbol in Hinduism and Buddhism. It is wielded by the god Shiva. Durga also holds a trishula, as one of her many weapons.

The Unclad God

There was a time I wanted to see
naked people.

Women—for obvious reasons.

Nude men affected me in many ways.
Every time I saw them
I became conscious of myself
followed by a comparative check.
If mine was shorter
I'd run to my workspace
and read a memo to myself.
It said size had nothing to do
with female orgasm.

Bare men reminded me
of my unkempt body hair,
how I had to trim and oil
to make it healthier.

Rituals

I don't look at unveiled people anymore.
It is either my age or hormones.
I now look beyond the flesh, bone and keratin.

I've been told
the finer body dwells undressed.

Promising Griefs

Neither the plow
nor the bankrupt farmer knows
whether the earth will receive
optimum water.

Consider the rice seed—
not sure if it will rejoice
sprouting into a plant
that will invariably die
to give us food for life.

Anyday

If wishes were horses, beggars would ride.

Should I stop daydreaming? With open eyes, I see events happen the way I want them to occur. They don't make me sweat, nor do they allow me to waste money I've been spending on movies. Unlike cinemas, they hardly create an atmosphere of make-believe. Daydreams are unconventional. I paint them in all colors and emerge as a champion. It's always a win-win situation that cannot be achieved in trance. I'm not Lord Shiva; marijuana doesn't help me envision aspirations in daylight. Daydreams allow monologues, design smiles on my lips. Blessed are the souls who daydream, for every moon has its share of nightmares.

The moments of harboring angst don't contribute to my reveries. They are regular leftovers of grim humors, the dusk writes across the world of faeries.

A Place Like Home

Lights turned off,
three glasses retire
as the bar closes.
The first stands upright,
the other upside down,
another lies horizontal.

For last few hours
the crystals held liquor,
ice, scent and comfort.
They also witnessed
eyes that spoke volumes
while lashes refused
to flutter.

The pub reopens
the next day
to the riff of unrest.

Sridevi

Your name hints at a goddess.
You endorse strength of will to the extent
that humans transform into snakes
and vice versa.

I wish you had taken away
all the venoms when you left.

Note: Reflecting on *Nagina*, a Hindi blockbuster, at the untimely demise of legendary Sridevi on Feb 24, 2018.

After the Book Fair

Their premises won't attract readers
anymore. Publishers, sellers, and a handful of
authors will spend hours packing
books and goods unsold. From the shelves,
new hope will follow the merchandise.
Apprehensions too will fill spaces in
the packs. A sense of relief prevails
over bargains.

Masala Muri

Ginger slices do not titillate
my taste-buds again.

The tangy golden mustard oil
does not tease my nostrils anymore.

Onions fail to dew my eyes now;
they were never kept in cold water
before Baba chopped them; while he got
his lenses damp, Ma had tears.

On every stormy Sunday
we invariably had power cuts,
and Baba cooked dinner for us all:

a moderate serving of Muri mixed with
onion, ginger and blobs of oil.

On such occasions, we used to sit close,
facing each other we shared our stories;
from airing endless grievances on our barren

curriculum, the dialogues on the utility
of learning Sanskrit,
to refuting Ma's advice on being courteous
even to strangers we would meet.

Our room shined in kerosene lamps.

Load-shedding no longer casts its spell;
the back-ups are prompt and steady
we order food—the mobile app comes handy,
but Muri seldom makes it to our monthly grocery.

The next monsoon I wish to buy
a new lantern,
and I'll light it once in a while
to accompany the old snack
and fresh stories in our family.

Note: Muri is a traditional Bengali snack, otherwise called puffed rice.

Faith

Rituals do not add to our credos.

Rakhi enlivens familial warmth
without religious fidelity. On
Eid seviyan is for all.

Patrons stand up in multiplexes
when the national anthem is relayed.

Indianness precedes theology.

Exhibition

I think of effigies with fractured noses.

Statuettes of gods, goddesses, kings, unmasked in
museums. Does this take
a toll on their pride?

Nature made the nasal frame fragile.
How do they breathe the vain air?

WATER HAS MANY COLORS

Year of Publication 2022
Publisher: Hawakal (New Delhi, Calcutta)
Illustration: Rochishnu Sanyal

CONTENTS

Spectrum **159** | Santiniketan **160** | Sepia **161** | The Bottle **162** | My Father Looks Like Me **163** | Line of Control **164** | Boris Johnson in Isolation **165** | Hibiscus **166** | Vernacular **168** | Troth **169** | Souvenir **170** | Orison **171** | Bucolic Bengal **172** | When a Woman Conquers God **174** | Urvashi—Beyond Her Siren Avatar **176** | Bhanurekha **177** | Lucency **179** | Coterie **180** | Intrinsic **181** | Monostichs **182** | Classic **183-189** | Why You Should Not Buy a Book **190** | Game **191** | Memoir **192** | Rosary **193**

Spectrum

Water has many colors,
smudging pebbles
along its path.

Santiniketan

Aesthetes preach Tagore.
Officials display replica of
the Nobel Prize.

Sepia

remembering Subhash Mukhopadhyay *on his birth centenary*

The teller has a way
to regale the crowd. He stops
as the princess turns into a witch
and wolfs him.

It's the same raconteur who fails
to amuse the audience
with his rendition of the river:

She makes him wait as she
rushes to the other end.
Time reminds him it will
never leave him alone.

What the narrator doesn't spill:
monarchs have several maws.
They chew; they don't even spare the creators.

The Bottle

Placed atop a garden lamp,
the container is empty.
Straw fails to diffuse
the flavor of beverage.

What does Jallianwala Bagh uphold?

Bullet marks on brick walls.
Blood and clots.
The 13th day of April in 1919.
Amar Jyoti—the imperishable light.

Does the ground stand
by the visitor who passes through security
to relish a drink
while reflecting on mass annihilation?

My Father Looks Like Me

This isn't unfounded.
If you think any other way, you are mistaken.
Hinting at his emission is scientific.
Other reasons will fall short.
I'm the one from the crowd:
the rest were lost.

No one ever keeps an account.
Look at me: I made him a parent.
The world claims Ma and I are identical.
They fail to notice she and Baba look alike.

Line of Control

Strays recognize the regulars.
Roadside tea stalls house a convoy of canines.
They chomp or chew as walk-ins stop by.
Owner of the kiosk discreetly suggests
the stuff the mutts cherish.

My stroll to the cha shop is routinely challenged.
Curs from the neighborhood march along.
Affray crams the air.

Boris Johnson in Isolation

With newsflashes, we're alerted—
policy warrants seclusion.
Kerfuffles over the microbe
leave us baffled: isn't there
any limit to its influence?

Officials are unruffled:
famine is meatier than the virus.
Religion spawns decimation.

Resources pledge welfare,
as quarantine breaks sequence.
Doesn't inanition evade all control?

Note: The UK Prime Minister tests positive with Coronavirus and goes into self-isolation, reports *The Guardian*.

Hibiscus

I've to leave.
As long as I'm alive,
I'll clean the muck off the earth.
My pledge to the newborn:
I must make the world livable for you.
     — Sukanta Bhattacharya*

1

The vow ceased with his death.
The world expanded.
They never missed a chance
to cram her to misery.
Can we be of help?

2

Feed the earth water
she flows in abundance.
Allow the planet to breathe:
the air is her consort.

Free her from plastics—
they choke progress.
She endures the mess
her wards make.

3

Can I become a tree?
As I rampart the sinew
with my root embedded
in her tissue, I'll bloom
like a hibiscus:
the blush will endorse
my bloodline.

4

Infestation ushers in
a day of buried majesty.
I wish the flower could turn
into a coral, basking in sunshine.
Mother awaits the levitating saint.

*An excerpt from Bhattacharya's celebrated Bengali poem "Chharpatra" ("Certificate of Exemption"), published in 1947. Translation is mine.

Vernacular

We can't find the source
when he wakes us from sleep.
Snivels are his lingo of wabbit.
Berceuses fail to dull him.
Pats on his posterior
offer no repose.

Infants latch onto a patois
that parents wish to recall.

Troth

Do you think that our love can create miracles? Do you think our love could take us away together?
—Allison Hamilton in *The Notebook*

Will my wife cross-examine me
as Allison did?
She wishes to depart first.
What if her yen is quashed?

She guards two pairs of bangles:
coral and conch.
Missus ensures they are intact.
She fears a chink will curtail my breath.

Note: Allison (aka Allie) is the protagonist of the 2004 American romantic drama film, *The Notebook*.

Souvenir

What is the lifespan of memory?
Until a mouser keeps calm, licking the milk bowl?
Or the snake woman mourns her partner?

In my case:
Ma's healing touch.
The tiepin from fiancée,
mortgaging gold.
Newborn glued to gut
flavors of the first liaison.

I cannot recollect the penultimate line
of her lyrics. Aging isn't linear.
It blights the keepsakes.

Orison

Vermilion marks her placing.
Blushing bride bows.

Elders exalt the esse of
her spouse—
Sada suhagan raho.

Note: *Sada suhagan raho* (be blessed with your husband) is a common way of blessing a newly married woman, usually by the elderly females of the Hindi/Urdu-speaking Indian families.

Bucolic Bengal

1

Crossovers recoup the breach
as water evokes
figures of fellowship.

2

Clay or cut—
frolics do not cease
over trifles. Riverside
hosts the young as
clouds burst into drizzles.

3

Kash reveals autumn.

Fisher plies shallop to
pluck the floating plenty.

4

Fancies fathom no ceiling.
Can iris assess the zenith?
Kites are born of chimeras.

5

Travelers gather around the Baul.
What does he chant?
Melody unfurls.

Govinda manifests
across the bank of Ajay.

6

Argil raises the hovel.
Bamboo and retted jute stem
mold to model.

The owl assures daughter
acts like the goddess.

7

Her gaze is fixed.
Mien limns the reality.

When a Woman Conquers God
after Manasamangal Kāvya

Hail Padmavati:
pardon my ignorance.

Brides in rural layouts
are reminded of Behula.
Her commitment and how hard-
ship failed to mute her ardor.
Onerous it was to fetch your
favor. Behula reifies devotion.
Legend stresses a laundress
ushered Behula to heaven
to revive her late spouse.

Derided for your limited vision,
you evoked fear of well-being.
You were granted the godhead
as Chand conceded to your ruse.

Did Behula claim indelible stature?

Did she ask for homage?
While believers observe Behula as
a loyal soulmate, you remained a deity
to be worshiped with the left hand.

Urvashi—Beyond Her Siren Avatar

1

The *Mahabharata* does not
ratify your fondness for Arjuna.
It must be severe when he
declined your plea.
Worthy was your forethought
as you imprecated him.

In his last year of living incog,
Arjuna turned into Brihannala.

2

Your son Rishysringa helped
Dasharatha become the father
of Rama.

Does the *Ramayana* endorse
your direction to Treta Yuga?

Bhanurekha

after Bhanurekha, *stage name* Rekha, *one of the divas of Indian cinema*

That I'm an aesthete and a Re-enthusiast prompts one to show curiosity: She is married, isn't she? Following Indian tradition, she wears vermilion! To this, I evoke her facade: *Red adds to her ebullience, but she is considered an excellent camouflage.*

That she dons golden conjeevaram and radiant fripperies for public appearances, my mentor describes her as a Christmas tree. I don't find it cynical; I address the concern: *Despite green needles, the tree is furnished with animated reveries.*

That admirers fail to detach her courtesan avatar from her real-life identity has nothing to do with the gajras she carries. I'm jealous: *The jasmines are lucky*!

That we hardly remember the initials of her first name does not prevent sunshine from falling for her. Looking at her middle parting, I find relief: *The Scalp should look ivory.*

She says she prefers being called mystique (but not mysterious) and intriguing (but not sexy). This helps refract her luminescence, and I spot the prism: *White has its share of density.*

Note: Bhanurekha is the union of two words: Bhanu (Sun) and Rekha (Line). It means sunbeam.

Lucency

I have a reason to suspect the vision when they say it is a kaleidoscopic world. Is it color deficiency? Textbook suggests that inadequacy lies with the cone cells. I doubt how many colors they can see! Does the earth become polychromatic only by envisioning a color or two? Then, why do we call it a red rose? We could have said it was a variegated blossom. Why do we refer to coal as black? Coal is psychedelic, rather! What about "milky white?" Milk is rainbow; correct me if I'm not right. How many hues have you envisaged so far? I ask about the hues, but not your bizarre way of depicting them. I figure out the similarities and differences between color and queerness. I also assess the tints of your eccentricity. They are red, yellow, or blue. I'm aware human beings, with all their strangeness, point at their feelings to describe colors. Laughter, wail, jealousy, grief, and joy: what are paints barring these sentiments? How can one describe the earth as varicolored? Let me ask: What is the color of deafness? How will you tinge a mute tree? Can you stain dumbness in any tint? Is clot the only color to portray the wounded genital of a woman? Does it not have male filth? The lesion also marks tears. You know, water is achromic and otherwise called life!

Coterie

The earth has grown plastic. Water takes eons to seep. The burnout of trees is due to blemished air. Neonates feed on supplements. Does frondescence succor wellbeing?

Air-conditioning helps appraise accommodation. Windowpanes don't open to the sky. Owners enhance décor with filament lights. A flame tree stands alone beside the gateway. Old leaves cover the passage.

Wood is abolished to expand highways. The flamboyant tree dies from Roman vitriol.

Intrinsic

I've been watching movies for years, and I don't remember when I first grabbed a popular film magazine. I became an avid reader of *Anandalok, Filmfare, Stardust,* and *Cine Blitz*. Did the actors discuss why they chose to become actors? They explained what they might have done otherwise. Someone could have become a lawyer, a doctor, an engineer, or a researcher in a specific science. We tend to think that the actors had no other career options. Clad in white, Simi Grewal questioned her guests: *How did you get your first break?* Cinema honors light.

Was Joy Goswami asked, *What if you weren't a poet?*

MONOSTICHS

Prayer

What if I am mute or loud?

COVID-19

Breathing banks on black market.

Mutual

Proximity is fatal.

Celebrations

Zero tolerance for outdoor missions.

Euphoria

Autumn, thy name is Mother.

CLASSIC

Ma

In the kitchen,
her bangles
play a carillon.

CLASSIC

Missus

My falling-out fails to furcate;
her silence, the shield.

CLASSIC

Baba

My son tumbles.
Get back
on your toes, I tell him.

CLASSIC

Housekeeper

Climbing the stairs,
he calls my mother.

His voice reverberates.

Laundryman is at the door.

CLASSIC

Paperboy

The buzzer chimes.

And a thumping sound
assures me of news-
paper.

From my balcony,
I spot the newsie
with his bicycle.

Moisture
graces his features.

CLASSIC

Colonial

Debates do not
alter biases.

Is it not apt
to slice edges
of the loaf
for a snack?

CLASSIC

Ho-Hum

How many times
do we learn
the same dicta?

Flyers will use
emergency exit
when pilot asks—
Evacuate…

Freedom arrives
with *Talaq…*

Priest winds up the rites,
invoking peace—
Om Shanti….

Why You Should Not Buy a Book

An opus is best avoided.
Author does not play in defense;
the cover spread often deceives.

The scribe isn't a teacher.
An insignificant title alerts us—
be prudent with nest eggs.

Game

Women arrive
with a pot of vermillion
as the goddess departs.

Memoir

for Mathures Paul

Lasting dilemma erupts
as a sapling
splits open concrete.

Does a dwelling
fear oblivion?

A tree proliferates.
It adds to antiquity.

Rosary

1

Pearls find a way
back to the oysters.

2

Keeping count
for a one-off.

3

Does clairvoyance
call for an add-on?

Can names lead me
to the anonymous?

Beads are tags,
they accept duality.

ONENESS

Year of Publication 2024
Publisher: Transcendent Zero Press (Houston, Texas)
Illustration: Rochishnu Sanyal

CONTENTS

haiku **199-204** | The Man in the Rain **205** | Primordial Leaning **206** | The Publisher and the Poet **207** | On Exit **208** | Separation **210** | Entitlement **211** | Equipoise **212**

Oneness

haiku

descent of grace
the priest unburdens
the donation box

haiku

full moon
across the landscape
fireflies

Oneness

haiku

the postbox
recedes to rust
the lost art

haiku

plagiarism
the author examines
the reader's memory

Oneness

haiku

wisdom
the third molar adds
to the surgeon's expertise

haiku

flowers nestle the landscape
springtide
the poet glimpses it regardless

(Remembering legendary Bengali poet Subhash Mukhopadhyay's iconic coinage—*Flowers bloom or not, it's springtime.*)

The Man in the Rain

Do I know him?
A man walks down the public road,
ignoring the thunderstorm.
He is alone—
downpour fails to wet him.

The gentleman looks composed.
Seeing him from a distance, I leave
the roadside shade. Incongruity guides
me to approach the stranger.

Drenched in the deluge,
I progress to catch him.
He briskly drifts away.
My cellphone beeps:

The weather forecast suggests
a day-long cloudburst.

Primordial Leaning

You define women as Durga or
Kali. Are you a believer? Are you
being kind? You could have convinced
them to fight the evil. Instead, when you
imply the goddess, do you illustrate
sisterhood with many limbs? Would you
like men to act as Shiva—the destroyer?

The Publisher and the Poet

When you admire my piece,
I flash a twinkle.

Unpredicted plaudit alerts me
to explore spam emails.

Submissions don't arrive
in my standard folder anymore.

When you call me a pro,
I notice you are eyeing

free books you can't claim.
When you designate me

corporate, I find you curious.
Do you assume the proceeds?

But when you find me impolite,
I sustain your objection.

I appreciate your skill
to navigate my air.

On Exit

1

Does grief know
its future?

Like the river,
it refuses to cease
but reveals progression.

2

Why do I fail
to prefix Late
with my father's name?

3

The family is aware of
my affinity for ghee.
They add a spoonful
to steamed rice, enticing
my appetite.

In the crematorium,
the priest asks me to
smear ghee on my
father's skin. He ensures
the fire finds Baba luscious.

4

When I floated his ashes
in the Ganges, I realized
my father's passage from
his bedroom to the crematory
was therapeutic.

Separation

Only a little needs to be invested
in sketching the worn-out tree.

A charcoal or two, canvas,
and span.

I place myself amid the landscape
to explain the prevailing isolation.

Entitlement

It is sufficient
if you call me Kiriti.
Grandparents bestowed
me with the forename. I wasn't
aware of it until I could talk. I didn't choose
my surname either; my parents weren't my choice.
Pet names insinuate ownership. They work best for the assignors.
It's vital to acquire the rights when one desires to name me distinctively.

Equipoise
for Sreenanda Shankar

It's interesting to notice
you appreciate restraint.
I noted your claim—
Can't think of a caption…
sometimes silence works.

Your portrait co-occurred,
conveying more than
the penned letters.

Quietude overwhelms.
Pictures register sonic
waves, stemming from
the surface and beneath,
otherwise unheard of.

NEW POEMS
(from 2024 to 2025)

Photograph: Bitan Chakraborty

CONTENTS

Violence **217** | Demonstration **218** | Fellowship **219** | Her Sacred Mist **220** | Photography **221** | Consciousness **222** | Durva **223** | Eulogy **225**

New Poems (2024-2025)

Violence

On my birthday,
Bitan genially offers
Rushdie's *Knife*.
He indites:
Not all daggers kill.

We were scared;
stabbing of the author
made to newsflashes
and debates. Investigations
unveiled a layered context.

Do all casualties stir the air?
At home or work, sufferers
seldom show signs of injury
when cutters flaunt the edges
of sucrose crystals.

Note: A sugar-coated knife (following the Bengali idiom, *Micchri- Chhuri*) hints at a sweet taste while actually lacerating someone's soul.

Demonstration
for the doctor, raped and killed on Aug 9 at RG Kar Medical College, Kolkata

Calling out misery
cannot assure justice.
Does rectitude
wake overnight?
Peccadillos create
routes to felonies.
Ages pass,
bringing the upright.

Death pauses the verdict;
authority mars evidence.
The doomed is put
on pyre; rallies slit
through the silence.

Monarch keeps a vigil,
foreseeing a mass mutiny.
Iniquity is ignored
as the records stand revised
for scrutiny.

Fellowship

As a born Hindu, it took me
a few months to be baptized.
But when I chose to practice
Islam, I was scared of circumcision,
believing it was a prerequisite. Eventually,
I learned this wasn't true, but until then,
I had willfully suppressed my wish.

Frequent newsbreaks alerted us
to the Pahalgam terrorist attack.
I was torn: Would I be happy not to
trust Allah? Or should I revive
my interest I once lost?

Innocent men who refused to read
Kalma-e-Shahadat were shot dead.
Before firing, they were forced to show
their genitals. Did the terrorists have
a foreskin fetish?

Faiths have failed to foster camaraderie.
Is altruism headed towards extinction?

Note: 26 people were killed after terrorists opened fire on tourists in Jammu and Kashmir on 22 April 2025. Chief Minister Omar Abdullah (Jammu and Kashmir) described the incident as "much larger than anything we've seen directed at civilians in recent years."

Her Sacred Mist

The daughter gleaned joy
for the past few days
amidst her parents and children.

When I woke up early,
the trees, the leaves,
and the grasses were damp.

The rising sun parched them
before late.
I probed the air:

Did the Mother weep as
she left for Kailash?
The wife returned to her spouse.

Note: Hindu mythology holds that Goddess Durga brings her children when she visits her paternal home annually in autumn. After a designated period, she returns to her husband, Shiva, at Mount Kailash.

New Poems (2024-2025)

Photography
for Raghu Rai

1

camerawork—
anticipating
the perfect moments

2

camerawork—
recounting
the stories

3

camerawork—
the eyelashes
freeze in place

Consciousness

> *My friend, you stand erect*
> *beyond the edge of life and death.*
> — Rabindranath Tagore

A friend asked,
Who would you talk to
among the deceased?

I had to be quick.

Several names
crammed my crown,
Dad's included.

I answered, *God.*

New Poems (2024-2025)

Durva
for Durba Chatterjee (DOB: 25 September 2023)

1
As I learn more about you,
I'll pick up a batch or two
wherever I reach.

2

The courtyard knew my boyhood days.
You embraced my unshod limbs
and healed my bruises as I slipped.

You made up the loving drape
the earth donned for my convenience.

3

You taught us harmony. Resting in your mesh
were the rice grains. Strengthened by prayers,
you sat on my scalp for the nuptials. The bride
held you in her hair.

4

You embody divine grace.
You are more pristine than water
that turns holy as it lets you sink.

5

You add to the sanctity of the soil.
Blessed are the humans raising you
in their yards.

Like Draupadi, the planet mourns
when the veil is withdrawn.

Note: Durva or Durba is a common Bengali name for girls. It denotes Bermuda or Conch grass, known for its many therapeutic properties and frequent use in Hindu rituals. Numerous Puranic stories are linked to Durva grass. In the *Mahabharata*, the Kauravas stripped Draupadi, subjecting her to great humiliation and distress.

Eulogy

Wish I could secure
a better place
for you.

I found you
at peace
here on earth.

Kiriti Sengupta, awarded the 2018 Rabindranath Tagore Literary Prize and the 2024 Nilim Kumar National Honor, has had his poetry published in various outlets, including *The Common*, *The Florida Review Online*, *Headway Quarterly*, *The Lake*, *Amethyst Review*, *Dreich*, *Moria Online*, *Otoliths*, *Outlook*, *The Chakkar*, *The Daily Star*, *Borderless Journal*, *Madras Courier*, and others. He has authored fourteen books of poetry and prose, published two volumes of translations, and edited nine anthologies. Sengupta is the chief editor of *Ethos Literary Journal* and heads the English division at Hawakal Publishers Private Limited, one of the leading independent presses founded by Bitan Chakraborty. He lives in New Delhi. More information is available at www.kiritisengupta.com.

Photograph Courtesy: Bitan Chakraborty

www.ingramcontent.com/pod-product-compliance
Lightning Source LLC
Chambersburg PA
CBHW060521080526
44586CB00012B/560